The Dorling Kindersley Book of Nursery Rhymes

Debi Gliori

DK

A Dorling Kindersley Book

Dorling DK Kindersley

London, New York, Munich,
Paris, Melbourne, Delhi

Project Editor Fiona Munro
Designers Laia Roses and Joanna Pocock
Senior Editor Marie Greenwood
Managing Art Editor Jacquie Gulliver
Managing Editor Joanna Devereux
DTP Designer Jill Bunyan **Production** Joanne Rooke

First published in Great Britain in 2000 by

Dorling Kindersley Limited,

A Penguin Company
80 Strand, London WC2R 0RL

A CIP catalogue record for this book is
available from the British Library.

ISBN: 0-7513-6695-1

Colour reproduction by Bright Arts
Printed in China by L. Rex
4 6 8 10 9 7 5
Acknowledgements
The publishers would like to thank the following
for their kind permission to reproduce their photographs:
Mary Evans Picture Library: pages 25 and 60

Additional photography by Jane Burton, Gordon Clayton, Philip Dowell,
Steve Gorton, Dave King, Will Ling, David Murray and Jules Selmes,
Susanna Price, Kim Sayer, Stephen Shott, Jerry Young.

see our complete
catalogue at
www.dk.com

The Dorling Kindersley Book of Nursery Rhymes

Debi Gliori

CONTENTS

INTRODUCTION

ILLUSTRATING THIS COLLECTION of nursery rhymes was very similar to sewing a patchwork quilt. I sat with a higgledy-piggledy pile of poems wondering how I was going to piece them together and make a book. Like patchwork, they needed a common thread to bind them together into a seamless whole.

My threads are threefold. The first weaves in and out of the poems – the book starts in the early morning, moves through the day and ends up tucked up at bedtime. The second is a family thread, three children that spend their days with Humpty Dumpty, feeding jam tarts to their dog. And then there is a brand new thread, woven out of my desire to make something new from these poems, some of which have been handed down through the generations for hundreds of years.

As in patchwork, some pieces refused to fit unless turned around, again and again, until I found a fresh way of telling an old story.

The poems have a rich and varied past, and are part of our cultural heritage. Our book dips into this with little snippets of information relating to the rhymes.

At last, the patchwork is complete, the threads knotted and tied. Just as a quilt is only a collection of pieces of cloth until it is spread over a bed and used, this book is just a book until you, the reader, pick it up and read it aloud. Then it comes to life, is shared with those we love and is given a voice. Then it becomes yours.

Debi Gliori

Girls and boys come out to play,
The moon doth shine as bright as day.
Leave your supper and leave your sleep,
And join your play fellows in the street.
Come with a whoop and come with a call,
Come with a good will or not at all.
Up the ladder and down the wall,
A half-penny loaf will serve us all;
You find milk, and I'll find flour,
And we'll have a pudding in half an hour.

This rhyme used to be sung in the evenings by children calling their friends out to play.

9

Humpty Dumpty sat on the wall,
Humpty Dumpty had a great fall.
All the king's horses and all the king's men
Couldn't put Humpty together again.

Humpty Dumpty was a game. The players would sit on the ground holding their knees, then fall backwards and try to stand up.

Hey diddle diddle,

The cat and the fiddle,
The cow jumped over the moon;
The little dog laughed
To see such sport,
And the dish ran away with the spoon.

Doctor Foster went to Gloucester

In a shower of rain;

He stepped in a puddle,

Right up to his middle,

And never went there again.

The old word for puddle was "piddle" which rhymed with middle.

It's raining, it's pouring,
The old man is snoring;
He went to bed
And bumped his head
And couldn't get up in the morning.

In the 1800s, when this poem was written, families living in the country would often raise lambs by hand and they would become pets.

Mary had a little lamb,
Its fleece was white as snow;
And everywhere that Mary went
The lamb was sure to go.

It followed her to school one day,
That was against the rule;
It made the children laugh and play
To see a lamb at school.

And so the teacher turned it out,
But still it lingered near,
And waited patiently about
Till Mary did appear.

Why does the lamb love Mary so?
The eager children cry;
Why, Mary loves the lamb, you know,
The teacher did reply.

Ride a cock-horse to Banbury Cross,
To see a fine lady upon a white horse;
Rings on her fingers and bells on her toes,
She shall have music wherever she goes.

In this rhyme a "cock-horse" probably meant a toy horse.

Yankee Doodle came to town,
Riding on a pony;
He stuck a feather in his cap
And called it macaroni.

Little Miss Muffet
Sat on a tuffet,
Eating her curds and whey;
Along came a spider,
Who sat down beside her,
And frightened Miss Muffet away.

Curds are what milk becomes before it is made into cheese. Whey is the watery part of milk.

Incy Wincy spider

Climbed up the water spout;
Down came the rain
And washed the spider out;
Out came the sunshine
And dried up all the rain;
Incy wincy spider
Climbed up the spout again.

Mary, Mary, quite contrary

Mary, Mary, quite contrary
How does your garden grow?
With silver bells and cockle shells
And pretty maids all in a row.

Ladybird, ladybird,

Fly away home,
Your house is on fire
And your children all gone;
All except one
And that's little Ann,
And she has crept under
The warming pan.

*It is unlucky
to harm a
ladybird. If one
lands on you, say
this rhyme to send
it away unharmed.*

Sing a song of sixpence,
A pocket full of rye;
Four-and-twenty blackbirds
Baked in a pie.
When the pie was opened
The birds began to sing;
Wasn't that a dainty dish
To set before the king?

The king was in his counting-house
Counting out his money;
The queen was in the parlour
Eating bread and honey.
The maid was in the garden
Hanging out the clothes,
When down flew a blackbird
And pecked off her nose.

The origins of this rhyme may lie in an Italian recipe from 1549. This was for a pie that, when opened revealed live birds.

Lavender's blue, diddle, diddle,
Lavender's green;
When I am king, diddle, diddle,
You shall be queen.

Call up your men, diddle, diddle,
Set them to work,
Some to the plough, diddle, diddle,
Some to the cart.

Some to make hay, diddle, diddle,
Some to thresh corn,
Whilst you and I, diddle, diddle,
Keep ourselves warm.

This song was originally known as a playful love song rather than a nursery rhyme.

I had a little nut tree,
Nothing would it bear
But a silver nutmeg
And a golden pear.

The King of Spain's daughter
Came to visit me,
And all for the sake
Of my little nut tree.

I skipped over water,
I danced over sea,
And all the birds in the air
Couldn't catch me.

Old King Cole

King Cole is a legendary figure who ruled in the third century.

Was a merry old soul,
And a merry old soul was he;
He called for his pipe,
And he called for his bowl,
And he called for his fiddlers three.
Every fiddler, he had a fiddle,
And a very fine fiddle had he;
Twee tweedle dee, tweedle dee,
    went the fiddlers.
Oh, there's none so rare
As can compare
With King Cole and his fiddlers three.

The Queen of Hearts

She made some tarts,
All on a summer's day;
The Knave of Hearts
He stole the tarts,
And took them clean away.

Pat-a-cake, pat-a-cake, baker's man,
Bake me a cake as fast as you can;
Pat it and prick it, and mark it with B,
And put it in the oven for baby and me.

Hot cross buns!

Hot cross buns!
One a penny, two a penny,
Hot cross buns!
If your daughters do not like them
Give them to your sons;
One a penny, two a penny,
Hot cross buns!

This rhyme was often sung by street sellers. Hot cross buns were traditionally eaten for breakfast on Good Friday.

Hickory, dickory, dock,
The mouse ran up the clock.
The clock struck one,
The mouse ran down,
Hickory, dickory, dock.

Children have chanted this rhyme for centuries. It was once used to decide who should go first in a game.

There was an old woman who lived in a shoe.
She had so many children she didn't know what to do.
She gave them some broth without any bread;
And whipped them all soundly and put them to bed.

Little Bo-Peep has lost her sheep,
And can't tell where to find them;
Leave them alone, and they'll come home,
Bringing their tails behind them.

Little Bo-Peep fell fast asleep,
And dreamt she heard them bleating;
But when she awoke, she found it a joke,
For they were still all fleeting.

Then up she took her little crook,
Determined for to find them;
She found them indeed, but it made her
    heart bleed,
For they'd left their tails behind them.

*Some think this rhyme
dates back to a hide-and-seek
game played by children in
the fourteenth century.*

It happened one day,
  as Bo-Peep did stray
Into a meadow hard by,
There she espied their tails side by side,
All hung on a tree to dry.

She heaved a sigh, and wiped her eye,
And over the hillocks went rambling,
And tried what she could, as a
  shepherdess should,
To tack each one to its lambkin.

Old Mother Hubbard

Went to the cupboard,
To fetch her poor dog a bone;
But when she came there
The cupboard was bare
        And so the poor dog
                had none.

She took a clean dish
To get him some tripe;
But when she came back
He was smoking a pipe.

She went to the alehouse
To get him some beer;
But when she came back
The dog sat in a chair.

She went to the tavern
For white wine and red;
But when she came back
The dog stood on his head.

She went to the fruiterer's
To buy him some fruit;
But when she came back
He was playing the flute.

She went to the tailor's
To buy him a coat;
But when she came back
He was riding a goat.

She went to the hatter's
To buy him a hat;
But when she came back
He was feeding the cat.

She went to the barber's
To buy him a wig;
But when she came back
He was dancing a jig.

She went to the cobbler's
To buy him some shoes;
But when she came back
He was reading the news.

She went to the seamstress
To buy him some linen;
But when she came back
The dog was a-spinning.

She went to the hosier's
To buy him some hose;
But when she came back
He was dressed in his clothes.

The dame made a curtsey,
The dog made a bow;
The dame said, Your servant,
The dog said, Bow-wow.

Pussy cat, pussy cat,
where have you been?
I've been to London to look for the queen.
Pussy cat, pussy cat, what did you there?
I frightened a little mouse under her chair.

It is believed that this rhyme tells of an incident that happened during the reign of Queen Elizabeth I.

36

I love little pussy,
Her coat is so warm,
And if I don't hurt her
She'll do me no harm.
So I'll not pull her tail,
Nor drive her away,
But pussy and I
Very gently will play.

She shall sit by my side,
And I'll give her some food;
And pussy will love me
Because I am good.

Peter Piper picked a peck of pickled pepper;
A peck of pickled pepper Peter Piper picked;
If Peter Piper picked a peck of pickled pepper,
Where's the peck of pickled pepper Peter Piper picked?

The pig that Tom stole and ate was not a real pig but a pastry pig filled with currants.

Tom, Tom, the piper's son,
Stole a pig and away did run;
The pig was eat, and Tom was beat,
Till he ran crying down the street.

When this rhyme was written, white bread was a refined food only eaten by the wealthy – quite a treat for Tommy!

Little Tommy Tucker

Sings for his supper;
What shall he eat?
White bread and butter;
How will he cut it,
Without a knife?
And how will he be married,
Without a wife?

Jack Sprat could eat no fat,
His wife could eat no lean;
And so, between them both,
They licked the platter clean.

Roses are red,
Violets are blue,
Sugar is sweet,
And so are you.

Little maid, pretty maid,

Whither goest thou?
Down in the forest to milk my cow.
Shall I go with thee?
No, not now.
When I send for thee
Then come thou.

Long ago, if you asked a girl to go milking with you, it was like asking her to marry you!

43

The three little kittens, they lost their mittens,
And they began to cry,
Oh, mother dear, we sadly fear,
That we have lost our mittens.
What! Lost your mittens, you naughty kittens!
Then you shall have no pie.
Meow, meow, meow,
No, you shall have no pie.

The three little kittens, they found their mittens,
And they began to cry,
Oh, mother dear, see here, see here,
For we have found our mittens.
Put on your mittens, you silly kittens,
And you shall have some pie.
Purr, purr, purr,
Oh, let us have some pie.

The three little kittens put on their mittens,
And soon ate up the pie;
Oh, mother dear, we greatly fear,
That we have soiled our mittens.
What! soiled your mittens, you naughty kittens!
Then they began to sigh,
Meow, meow, meow,
Then they began to sigh.

The three little kittens, they washed their mittens,
And hung them out to dry;
Oh! mother dear, do you not hear,
That we have washed our mittens?
What! washed your mittens, then you're good kittens,
But I smell a rat close by.
Meow, meow, meow,
We smell a rat close by.

Polly put the kettle on,
Polly put the kettle on,
Polly put the kettle on,
We'll all have tea.

Sukey take it off again,
Sukey take it off again,
Sukey take it off again,
They've all gone away.

Pease pudding hot,
Pease pudding cold,
Pease pudding in the pot
Nine days old.

This rhyme is a clapping song, sung on chilly days to keep cold hands warm. Pease pudding is a thin soup made from mashed peas.

Ring-a-ring o' roses,
A pocket full of posies;
A-tishoo! A-tishoo!
We all fall down!

It is a popular belief that this rhyme dates back to the Great Plague. A ring-shaped, rosy-coloured rash being a symptom.

See-saw, Margery Daw,

Jacky shall have a new master;
He shall have but a penny a day,
Because he can't work any faster.

49

The character Jack Horner first appeared in a book printed in the 18th century, in which he is only 13 inches tall!

Little Jack Horner

Sat in the corner,
Eating a Christmas pie;
He put in his thumb,
And pulled out a plum,
And said, "What a good boy am I!"

Jack and Jill went up the hill,
To fetch a pail of water;
Jack fell down and broke his crown,
And Jill came tumbling after.

Up Jack got, and home did trot,
As fast as he could caper,
To old Dame Dob, who patched his head
With vinegar and brown paper.

There was a crooked man,
and he walked a crooked mile,
He found a crooked sixpence against a crooked stile;
He bought a crooked cat, which caught a crooked mouse,
And they all lived together in a little crooked house.

Jack be nimble,
Jack be quick,
Jack jump over
The candlestick.

It was once believed that if you could jump over a candle without putting out the flame, you would have good luck for a year!

Monday's child is fair of face,
Tuesday's child is full of grace,
Wednesday's child is full of woe,
Thursday's child has far to go,
Friday's child is loving and giving,
Saturday's child works hard for a living,
But the child that is born on the Sabbath day,
Is bonny and blithe and good and gay.

One for sorrow,

Two for joy,

Three for a girl,

Four for a boy,

Five for silver,

Six for gold,

Seven for a secret ne'er to be told.

If you ever see magpies, you must recite this verse as you count them – you will often see more than one at a time.

Wee Willie Winkie runs through the town,
Upstairs and downstairs in his night gown,
Rapping at the window, crying through the lock,
Are the children all in bed, for now it's eight o'clock?

Hush little baby, don't say a word,
Papa's gonna buy you a mockingbird.

And if that mockingbird won't sing,
Papa's gonna buy you a diamond ring.

And if that diamond ring turns to brass,
Papa's gonna buy you a looking glass.

And if that looking glass gets broke,
Papa's gonna buy you a billy goat.

And if that billy goat won't pull,
Papa's gonna buy you a cart and bull.

And if that cart and bull turn over,
Papa's gonna buy you a dog named Rover.

And if that dog named Rover won't bark,
Papa's gonna buy you a horse and cart.

And if that horse and cart fall down,
You'll still be the sweetest little baby in town!

T winkle, twinkle, little star,
How I wonder what you are!
Up above the world so high,
Like a diamond in the sky.

When the blazing sun is gone,
When he nothing shines upon,
When you show your little light,
Twinkle, twinkle, all the night.

*A comic version
of this popular rhyme is
sung by the Mad Hatter
in Lewis Carroll's Alice's
Adventures in Wonderland.*

Sleep, baby, sleep,
Thy father guards the sheep;
Thy mother shakes the dreamland tree
And from it fall sweet dreams for thee,
Sleep, baby, sleep.

Sleep, baby, sleep,
Our cottage vale is deep;
The little lamb is on the green,
With woolly fleece so soft and clean –
Sleep, baby, sleep.

Sleep, baby, sleep,
Down where the woodbines creep;
Be always like the lamb so mild,
A kind and sweet and gentle child,
Sleep, baby, sleep.

Index of First Lines